Grief Journal

RESPOND TO THE REACTION
TO BE RESTORED

Mission: To Proclaim Transformation and Truth
Publisher: Transformed Publishing, Cocoa, FL
Website: www.transformedpublishing.com
Email: transformedpublishing@gmail.com

Cover, interior, and accent images were retrieved by the publisher, via paid subscription / terms of use from Storyblocks.

This work is based on the author's life experiences and personal Biblical study, prayer, and inspiration of the Holy Spirit. The intention of the author is to share her testimony, insight, and strategies which have helped her, in hope to inspire others. Any resemblance to someone else's life experiences, teaching, actual events or locales or persons, living or dead, is entirely coincidental. Author obtained the permission of others who contributed their testimonies to her work.

Unless otherwise indicated, Scripture quotations are taken from the New King James Version®. Copyright © 1982 by Thomas Nelson. Used by permission. All rights reserved.

ISBN: 978-1-953241-84-9 (paperback)
ISBN: 978-1-953241-85-6 (hardcover)

Grief Journal

RESPOND TO THE REACTION TO BE RESTORED

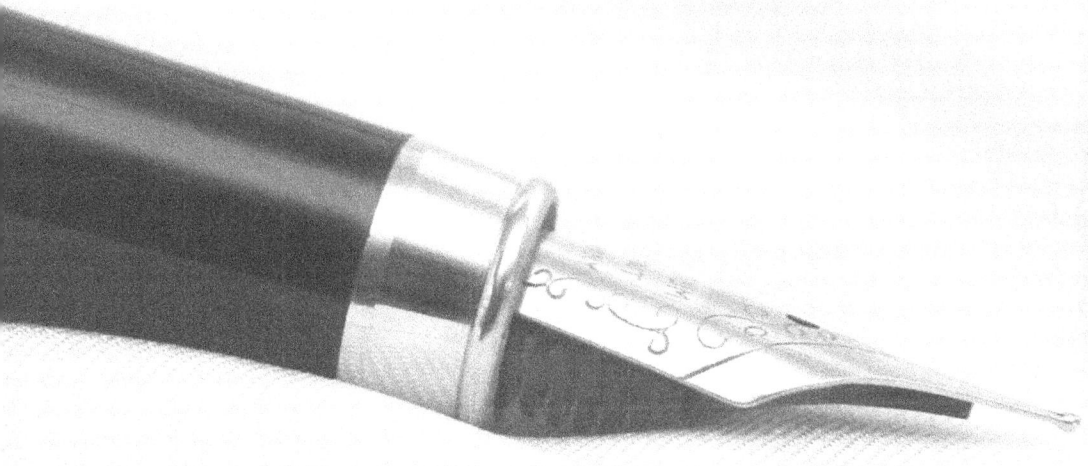

Denitrius Knowles

You number my wanderings;
Put my tears into Your bottle;
Are *they* not in Your book?
-Psalm 56:8

Dedication

To my parents,
Richard and Maxine Knowles,
who both departed this earth
on the sixteenth of November.
Dad in 2003 & Mom in 2017.

Nov. 16th

Table of Contents

My Personal Grief Story

I was born into a middle class married household. I was raised with four siblings (two brothers and two sisters) with me being the youngest of five children. We grew up as a close knit family who enjoyed spending holidays, birthdays, and special occasions together. Sunday dinners were the best and special to each one of us. My mom cooked big meals and the whole neighborhood ate. My dad, the gentle giant, was a true testament of a father. He took care of us, he showed us how to be productive men and women in society. Although both of my parents worked outside of the home, we never wanted or lacked anything. Love, food, finances, clothing, we had it all. To me, my parents were the best in the world.

My personal grief journey started on November 16, 2003 when I lost my first love, my protector, my gentle giant, my father Richard A Knowles. This was the first major loss I ever experienced in my life. I was somewhat prepared because I saw his decline, but you can never prepare for death. In the passing months, which became years, I dealt with his death by keeping busy; working, caring for my kids and my mother, overall, just being a *busy bee*. I did not process and respond to the encroaching grief. It *seemed* as time went on it became easier, but I know I was only suppressing it. I continued to push forward for my mother and my kids.

It appeared as if all was well for the next ten years or so, until I noticed a decline in my mother's health. For the next four years, I watched her health fade. I knew I must get ready for what was coming. Although I didn't know when, I knew it was inevitable. Around 2012, I started focusing more on my journey with the Lord. At that time, I did not know, He was preparing me for what was to come in the near future.

Under the teaching of Pastor Errol Beckford and Pastor Diana Robinson at Celebration Tabernacle Church in Cocoa, Florida, my faith and prayer life were strengthened and tested. The further I advanced in my walk with Christ, the more my heart and soul became rooted and firmly grounded. As I'm learning, by being taught the word of God and praying, I'm watching my mother's health weaken, yet still her faith never wavered. In this, I also gained strength from her. Despite bouts with continual pain and hospital stays, she never gave up.

November 2017, my mother's life changed for the worse. She was discharged from a critical hospitalization on November 9th. I picked her up and brought her home, only to have to call 911 within about two hours. She had a heart attack in my arms. The last words I heard my mother say to me were, "Please don't be angry with me!" At that time, I didn't realize she was telling me that she was leaving me. I knew she was gone when they rushed her away in the ambulance. She never returned home. She was kept alive on machines for a week.

That Thursday night was one of the hardest days of my life, I wrestled with the *whys* and *how could she*, until the Lord gave me peace late in the midnight hour. I woke up Friday with a renewed spirit, a new mindset, and ready to face life again. Fast forward to November 16th, the day the decision was made to remove my mom from all machines. My mother Maxine D. Knowles passed on November 16, 2017, the same month and day, exactly fourteen years after my father.

My grief process for my mother was much different than it was for my father. I was in a much different place in my walk with the Lord. I am the first to say, "I know it is no one but the Lord who carries me through this grief process." My mother was/is my heart, my everything, my backbone, my supporter, my biggest cheerleader. I was able to make her funeral arrangements, speak at her service, and encourage my family, but only by His Grace & Mercy!

I encourage everyone to grow in their personal relationship with the Lord. He is truly your strong tower, your comforter, your mother when you're motherless, your father when you're fatherless, your healer, your protector . . . I can go on and on. If you don't take anything else from this, please hear me when I say, "Try Jesus because He works!" I share this book, in loving memory of my father Richard A. Knowles and my Mother Maxine D. Knowles!

Blessings,
Denitrius "Niecy" Knowles

What is Grief?

Grief (n.) - a: deep and poignant distress caused by
or as if by bereavement
b: a cause of such suffering[1]

By definition, grief is characterized as strong feelings of distress, related to bereavement, which cause suffering. Grief is an emotional reaction and can trigger physical manifestations.

Emotions fluctuate based on our perspectives, shaped by past experiences and current circumstances. Physical death is a reality for everyone and every thing that lives. In fact, anything of the earth that can not die, is not classified as living. Death is the final stage of our journey on earth and enters us into eternity.

Thankfully, emotions are subject to change. God counsels us through His Word, teaching us to appropriately respond to initial reactions. We must be transformed from reacting (where our emotions dictate our actions) to responding (where principles lead our actions).

By design, humans are emotional. Emotions are not bad. However, emotions were never intended to be our final authority. Reactions to grief range from suppressing it to being suffocated by it. Knowing this, we must learn how to respond to our reactions to be restored.

[1]Merriam-Webster. "Definition of GRIEF." Merriam-Webster.com, 2019, www.merriam-webster.com/dictionary/grief.

I have both suppressed grief and been suffocated by it; back and forth and everything in between.

When I became proactive and started to navigate my grief, I found myself more grateful for what I had than bitter about what I lost. I realized every day apart, is a day closer to our reunion in heaven. I accepted the fact that everyone dies, I will too one day, and while present on the earth, I am the only one who can live the life God designed for me. I must fulfill my days and my design; benefit from the contributions of those who departed before me; and be beneficial to those who are coming after me.

When preparing for death and the transition of assets, we are prompted to list our beneficiary. More than the transfer of things, we must pour out love, godly attributes, and the inheritance of faith in God, for our loved ones to reference as they move forward through the challenges of life.

After I suffered for awhile, I learned to not allow grief to overtake me. When the emotions come, I found responses that work for me, and through this book, I am sharing the concepts with you.

But may the God of all grace, who called us to His eternal glory by Christ Jesus, after you have suffered a while, perfect, establish, strengthen, and settle *you*.

-1 Peter 5:10

Grief
Journal

Date: _____   Entry 1

<u>Daily Quote</u>:
Grief changes shape, but it never ends.
-Keanu Reeves[1]

<u>Activity</u>:
Write down your thoughts and feelings
about the loss of your loved one.

_____

_____

_____

_____

_____

_____

_____

_____

_____

_____

_____

_____

_____

_____

_____

_____

_____

_____

The Lord is near to those who have
a broken heart, and saves such as
have a contrite spirit.
-Psalm 34:18

Date: _____

<u>Daily Quote</u>:
Death leaves a heartache no one can heal,
love leaves a memory no one can steal.
-Richard Puz[2]

<u>Activity:</u>
Write a letter to your loved one.
Express unspoken feelings and communicate
anything you wish you could have said to them.

Blessed *are* those who mourn,
For they shall be comforted.
-Matthew 5:4

Date: _____   Entry 3

Daily Quote:
When someone you love becomes a memory,
the memory becomes a treasure.
-Anonymous[3]

Activity:
Create art in your loved one's memory.
(ie: pictures, drawings, blankets, etc.)

["]And God will wipe away every tear from their eyes; there shall be no more death, nor sorrow, nor crying. There shall be no more pain, for the former things have passed away."
-Revelation 21:4

Date: _____

To live in hearts we leave behind is not to die.
-Thomas Campbell[4]

Activity:
Create a memory box:
collect items that remind you of your loved one.

He heals the brokenhearted
And binds up their wounds.
-Psalm 147:3

Date: _____   Entry 5

Grief is the price we pay for love.
-Queen Elizabeth II[5]

Activity:
Go for a walk and remember the good
times you shared with your loved one.

["]These things I have spoken to you,
that in Me you may have peace. In the world
you will have tribulation; but be of good cheer,
I have overcome the world."
-John 16:33

Daily Quote:

There are three needs of the griever: To find the words for the loss, to say the words aloud, and to know that the words have been heard.
-Victoria Alexander[6]

Activity:

Honor your loved one by cooking their favorite dish or wearing their favorite color.

['] Fear not, for I *am* with you;
Be not dismayed, for I *am* your God.
I will strengthen you,
Yes, I will help you,
I will uphold you with My righteous right hand.'
-Isaiah 41:10

Date: _____   Entry 7

Daily Quote:
Grieving is a necessary passage and a difficult
transition to finally letting go of sorrow
-it is not a permanent rest stop.
-Dodinsky[7]

Activity:
Do an activity you and your loved one
used to do together.

[C]asting all your care upon Him,
for He cares for you.
-1 Peter 5:7

Date: _____   Entry 8

Daily Quote:
If tears could build a stairway and memories
a lane, I'd walk right up to heaven
and bring you home again.
-Author Unknown[8]

Activity:
Meditate: Allow yourself to sit in your feelings,
it's okay, just don't stay there.

"Then shall the virgin rejoice in the dance,
And the young men and the old, together;
For I will turn their mourning to joy,
Will comfort them,
And make them rejoice rather than sorrow.["]
-Jeremiah 31:13

Date: _____   Entry 9

<u>Daily Quote</u>:
Although it's difficult today to see beyond
the sorrow, may looking back in memory
help comfort you tomorrow.
-Author Unknown[9]

<u>Activity:</u>
Create a 'new normal' routine
you enjoy and stick to it.

Rejoice with those who rejoice,
and weep with those who weep.
Be of the same mind toward one another.
Do not set your mind on high things,
but associate with the humble.
Do not be wise in your own opinion.
-Romans 12:15-16

Date: _____   Entry 10

<u>Daily Quote</u>:
Grief is itself a medicine.
-William Cowper[10]

<u>Activity:</u>
Create a self-care plan:
Begin to engage in the things you love again.

Why are you cast down, O my soul?
And why are you disquieted within me?
Hope in God;
For I shall yet praise Him,
The help of my countenance and my God.
-Psalm 42:11

Date: _____   Entry 11

Daily Quote:
You cannot prevent the birds of sorrow from
flying over your head, but you can prevent
them from building a nest in your hair.
-Chinese Proverb[11]

Activity:
Listen to music that calms you,
yet brings you joy.

["]Come to Me, all *you* who labor and are
heavy laden, and I will give you rest.
Take My yoke upon you and learn from Me,
for I am gentle and lowly in heart,
and you will find rest for your souls.
For My yoke *is* easy and My burden is light."
-Matthew 11:28-30

Date: _____   Entry 12

Daily Quote:
Grief can't be shared. Everyone carries it alone,
his own burden in his own way.
-Anne Morrow Lindbergh[12]

Activity:
Write heartfelt notes of gratitude
and give them to family and friends.

I can do all things through
Christ who strengthens me.
-Philippians 4:13

Date: _____   Entry 13

Daily Quote:
You can clutch the past so tightly to your
chest that it leaves your arms too
full to embrace the present.
-Jean Gildewell[13]

Activity:
Journal using the prompt:
If I could change things, I would _____.

Therefore you now have sorrow;
but I will see you again and your heart will
rejoice, and your joy no one will take from you.
-John 16:22

Date: _____ Entry 14

<u>Daily Quote</u>:
No farewell words were spoken,
no time to say goodbye you were gone before
we knew it, and only God knows why.
-Author Unknown[14]

<u>Activity</u>:
Journal using the prompt:
Since the death of my loved one,
my family doesn't _____.
How does this make you feel?

My flesh and my heart fail;
But God is the strength of my heart
and my portion forever.
-Psalm 73:26

Date: _____   Entry 15

<u>Daily Quote</u>:
Perhaps there are not stars in the sky,
but rather openings where our loved ones
shine down to let us know they are happy.
-Eskimo Proverbs[15]

<u>Activity</u>:
Create a piece of jewelry with
your loved ones name on or inside of it.

For I consider that the sufferings of this present
time are not worthy *to be compared* with the
glory which shall be revealed in us.
-Romans 8:18

Daily Quote:
Dying is nothing to fear. It can be the
most wonderful experience of your life.
It all depends on how you've lived.
-Dr. Elisabeth Kubler-Ross[16]

Activity:
Create a special area in your
home to honor your loved one.

Peace I leave with you, My peace I give to you;
not as the world gives do I give to you. Let not
your heart be troubled, neither let it be afraid.
-John 14:27

Date: _____

Daily Quote:
A ton of regret never makes
an ounce of difference.
-Grenville Kleiser[17]

Activity:
Create a recipe book of the things
your loved one loved to cook
(or find out more about a hobby they enjoyed).

But I do not want you to be ignorant, brethren,
concerning those who have fallen asleep,
lest you sorrow as others who have no hope.
-1 Thessalonians 4:13

Date: _____   Entry 18

Daily Quote:
I still miss those I loved who are no longer with me,
but I find I am grateful for having loved them.
The gratitude has finally conquered the loss.
-Rita Mae Brown[18]

Activity:
Choose to grieve *and* heal.
It's okay to grieve, just don't stay there.

For if we believe that Jesus died and rose again,
even so God will bring with Him those
who sleep in Jesus.
-1 Thessalonians 4:14

Date: _____

<u>Daily Quote</u>:
People touch our lives if only for a moment.
And yet we're not the same from that moment on,
the time is not important, the moment is forever.
-Fern Bork[19]

<u>Activity</u>:
Communicate and Consider:
Express your needs and find acceptable
solutions to your grieving and healing process.

For this we say to you by the word of the Lord,
that we who are alive *and* remain until the
coming of the Lord will by no means
precede those who are asleep.
-1 Thessalonians 4:15

Date: _____

Daily Quote:
Our grief is as individual as our lives.
-Dr. Elisabeth Kubler-Ross[20]

Activity:
Connect - do not isolate.
Find a support group or spend time with
other family members or friends.

For the Lord Himself will descend from
heaven with a shout, with the voice of an
archangel, and with the trumpet of God.
And the dead in Christ will rise first.
-1 Thessalonians 4:16

Date: _____   Entry 21

Daily Quote:
Honest listening is one of the best medicines
we can offer the dying and the bereaved.
-Jeanie Cameron[21]

Activity:
Journal Prompt:
Something I love about my loved one.

Then we who are alive *and* remain shall be
caught up together with them in the
clouds to meet the Lord in the air.
And thus we shall always be with the Lord.
-1 Thessalonians 4:17

Date: _____

<u>Daily Quote</u>:
Say not in grief: 'He is no more',
but live in thankfulness that he was.
-Hebrew Proverb[22]

<u>Activity</u>:
Journal Prompt:
My loved one was proud of me because _ _ _ _ _.
How did that make you feel?

Therefore comfort one another with these words.
-1 Thessalonians 4:18

Daily Quote:
Life is not the way it is supposed to be,
it is the way it is.
The way you cope with it is
what makes the difference.
-Virginia Satir[23]

Activity:
Journal about the things you wish you
told your loved one before they died.

Surely He has borne our griefs
And carried our sorrows;
Yet we esteemed Him stricken,
Smitten by God, and afflicted.
-Isaiah 53:4

Date: _____

Daily Quote:
I will welcome happiness because it enlarges my heart; yet I will endure sadness because it opens my soul. I will acknowledge rewards because they are my due; yet I will welcome obstacles because they are my challenge.
-Og Mandino[24]

Activity:
Journal about ways you can adjust to the world without your loved one.

But He *was* wounded for our transgressions,
He was bruised for our iniquities;
The chastisement for our peace *was* upon Him,
And by His stripes we are healed.
-Isaiah 53:5

Date: _____

<u>Daily Quote</u>:
Some people come in your life as blessings.
Some come in your life as lessons.
-Mother Teresa[25]

<u>Activity</u>:
Jot down your triggers and recognize them i.e.:
when you smell their favorite fragrance,
or hear their favorite song.

All we like sheep have gone astray;
We have turned, every one, to his own way;
And the Lord has laid on Him the iniquity of us all.
-Isaiah 53:6

Date: _____

The best and most beautiful things in the
world cannot be seen or even touched
- they must be felt with the heart.
-Helen Keller[26]

Activity:
What is denial?
Did you go through denial?
If so, how did (or can) you overcome it?

["]Have I not commanded you?
Be strong and of good courage; do not be afraid,
nor be dismayed, for the Lord your God is
with you wherever you go."
-Joshua 1:9

Date: _____   Entry 27

Daily Quote:
We do not have to rely on memories to recapture
the spirit of those we have loved and lost
- they live within our souls in some perfect
sanctuary which even death cannot destroy.
-Nan Witcomb[27]

Activity:
What is anger?
Did you go through anger?
If so, how did (or can) you overcome it?

And we know that all things work together for good to those who love God, to those who are the called according to *His* purpose.
-Romans 8:28

Date: _____

<u>Daily Quote</u>:
Nurture yourself like you would anybody
else going through something this hard.
-Melvina Young[28]

<u>Activity:</u>
Document how you express
your emotions through this grief process.

To everything *there* is a season,
A time for every purpose under heaven:
A time to be born,
And a time to die;
A time to plant,
And a time to pluck *what* is planted;
-Ecclesiastes 3:1-2

Date: _____   Entry 29

Little by little, we let go of loss, but never love.
-Author Unknown[29]

Activity:
Identify your support team.
Who is helping you through these times?
Jot their names down and how they support you.

A time to kill,
And a time to heal;
A time to break down,
And a time to build up;
A time to weep,
And a time to laugh;
A time to mourn,
And a time to dance;
-Ecclesiastes 3:3-4

Date: _____   Entry 30

<u>Daily Quote</u>:
In quiet moments, may healing begin.
In broken places, may brightness shine in.
-Keely Chace[30]

<u>Activity:</u>
Learn to talk about your loss
and how it made you feel.
Write down your feelings to reflect,
always consider your support team.

A time to cast away stones,
And a time to gather stones;
A time to embrace,
And a time to refrain from embracing;
A time to gain,
And a time to lose;
A time to keep,
And a time to throw away;
-Ecclesiastes 3:5-6

Date: _____

<u>Daily Quote</u>:
There is no "normal" way to grieve.
Except for how we each do it.
-Melvina Young[31]

<u>Activity</u>:
Go and visit the grave or the place the
ashes of your loved one were released.
Bring flowers or another expression of love.

A time to tear,
And a time to sew;
A time to keep silence,
And a time to speak;
A time to love,
And a time to hate;
A time of war,
And a time of peace.
-Ecclesiastes 3:7-8

Date: _____   Entry 32

Lost in the wilderness of grief,
we seek our own paths to healing.
-Melvina Young[32]

Activity:
What do you have to say to your loved one today?

_____

_____

_____

_____

_____

_____

_____

_____

_____

_____

_____

_____

_____

_____

_____

_____

_____

_____

_____

_____

_____

_____

For I am persuaded that neither death nor life,
nor angels nor principalities nor powers,
nor things present nor things to come,
nor height, nor depth,
nor any other created thing shall be able
to separate us from the love of God,
which is in Christ Jesus our Lord.
-Romans 8:38-39

Date: _____

Daily Quote:
We wouldn't miss them so much
if we didn't love them so much.
-Meghan Craig[33]

Activity:
Share memories with others about your loved one.
Jot down some memories and reflect.

And above all things have
fervent love for one another,
for "love will cover multitude of sins."
-1 Peter 4:8

Date: _____

<u>Daily Quote</u>:
There is no timeline for grief,
no template for healing, no guideposts to follow.
There is only our heart letting us know when
we're ready to heal in our own way and time.
-Melvina Young[34]

<u>Activity of your choice:</u>

Write out a Scripture that is meaningful to you.

_____

_____

_____

Date: _____

<u>Daily Quote</u>:
To have strong feelings is what living and loving
are all about. It's all right to go on remembering
and missing someone who meant so much.
-Barb Loots[35]

<u>Activity of your choice:</u>

Write out a Scripture that is meaningful to you.

_____

_____

_____

About the Author

Denitrius Knowles became a mother in 1994; a child welfare worker in 2003, serving and advocating for one of the most vulnerable populations; and continues to be a pillar in her family from birth.

She understands the profound impact of loss. This journal was birthed from her own experiences while navigating a life of grief after the loss of her father in 2003 and her mother in 2017. Denitrius found journaling to be a vital tool for processing pain, making sense of the experience, and eventually rediscovering hope.

Her hope is that by sharing this journal others can navigate through similar losses and find comfort, feel less alone, and create their own safe space for healing.

Please contact Denitrius "Niecy" Knowles to share your testimony, request bulk book orders, to participate in upcoming book clubs. or schedule speaking engagements.

Social Media Tag: Niecy Knowles

Email:
griefjournalbrevardfl@gmail.com

Endnotes

[1] Reeves:, Keanu. "The Socratic Method." The Socratic Method, 18 Feb. 2024, www.socratic-method.com/quote-meanings-interpretations/keanu-reeves-grief-changes-shape-but-it-never-ends. Accessed 8 Jan. 2026.

[2] "22 Quotes about Grief to Comfort You When You Need It Most." Elite Daily, 2 Oct. 2017, www.elitedaily.com/p/22-quotes-about-grief-to-comfort-you-when-you-need-it-most-2755257. Accessed 8 Jan. 2026.

[3] Team, Editorial. "Top 50 Quotes about Love and Loss to Remember Loved Ones." Saint DiamondsTM, 27 Nov. 2024, saintdiamonds.com/blog/top-50-quotes-about-love-and-loss-to-remember-loved-ones/. Accessed 8 Jan. 2026.

[4] Poetryexplorer.net, 2026, www.poetryexplorer.net/poem.php?id=10024224#google_vignette. Accessed 8 Jan. 2026.

[5] https://www.facebook.com/InStyle. ""Grief Is the Price We Pay for Love" and 19 Other Unforgettable Queen Elizabeth Quotes." InStyle, 2025, www.instyle.com/queen-elizabeth-best-quotes-inspiration-11868035. Accessed 8 Jan. 2026.

[6] Downs, Chase. "10 Powerful Quotes about Grief to Share with Those in Need." Gather, 18 Oct. 2023, gather.app/blog/10-powerful-quotes-about-grief/.

[7] "Grief Quotes to Help You Find Comfort after a Loss | BetterHelp." Betterhelp.com, 2024, www.betterhelp.com/advice/grief/grief-quotes-to-help-you-find-comfort-after-a-loss/. Accessed 8 Jan. 2026.

[8] "If Tears Could Build..." Bestfriendmemorial.com, 2026, www.bestfriendmemorial.com/iftears.htm. Accessed 8 Jan. 2026.

[9] The Gardens. "15 Best Sympathy Quotes for Passings." The Gardens, 11 Sept. 2018, www.thegardens.com/best-sympathy-quotes-passings/. Accessed 8 Jan. 2026.

[10] "William Cowper Quote." Lib Quotes, 2017, libquotes.com/william-cowper/quote/lbb3g8q#google_vignette. Accessed 8 Jan. 2026.
Good News Network. "Chinese Proverb on Worrying." Good News Network, 23 Sept. 2025, www.goodnewsnetwork.org/that-the-birds-of-worry-fly-above-your-head-this-you-cannot-change-but-that-they-build-nests-in-your-hair-this-you-can-prevent-chinese-proverb/. Accessed 8 Jan. 2026.

[11] Lindbergh, Anne Morrow. "Anne Morrow Lindbergh Quote." FixQuotes, 10 Mar. 2012, fixquotes.com/quotes/grief-cant-be-shared-everyone-carries-it-alone-138148.htm. Accessed 8 Jan. 2026.

[12] Mills, Jonathan. "Get out of the Past Tense | Stretch for Growth." Stretch for Growth, 5 May 2024, www.stretchforgrowth.com/personal-development/get-out-of-the-past-tense/. Accessed 8 Jan. 2026.

[13] "If Tears Could Build a Stairway | Lily Mae Foundation." Lily Mae Foundation, 2025, www.lilymaefoundation.org/if-tears-could-build-a-stairway. Accessed 8 Jan. 2026.

[14] The. "22 Famous Eskimo Proverbs." Listofproverbs.com, 7 Jan. 2026, www.listofproverbs.com/source/e/eskimo_proverb/. Accessed 8 Jan. 2026.

[15] "Elisabeth Kubler-Ross Quotes about Dying | A-Z Quotes." A-Z Quotes, 2026, www.azquotes.com/author/8304-Elisabeth_Kubler_Ross/tag/dying. Accessed 8 Jan. 2026.

[16] "Grenville Kleiser Quote." A-Z Quotes, 2026, www.azquotes.com/quote/919880#google_vignette. Accessed 8 Jan. 2026.

[17] "Grief Quotes to Help You Find Comfort after a Loss | BetterHelp." Betterhelp.com, 2024, www.betterhelp.com/advice/grief/grief-quotes-to-help-you-find-comfort-after-a-loss/.

[18] "30 Sympathy Quotes to Share with Someone Grieving a Loss." TODAY.com, 4 Oct. 2022, www.today.com/life/quotes/sympathy-quotes-rcna47761.

[19] "Grief Counseling | Rewire and Restore." Rewire and Restore , 2024, www.rewireandrestore.com/grief. Accessed 8 Jan. 2026.

[20] "Jeanie (Jenny) Cameron Quote." A-Z Quotes, 2026, www.azquotes.com/quote/583077#google_vignette. Accessed 8 Jan. 2026.

[21] Meleen, Michele. "Cherishing Lost Loved Ones through Memorable Sayings." LoveToKnow, 28 Feb. 2011, www.lovetoknow.com/life/grief-loss/memorial-death-sayings. Accessed 8 Jan. 2026.

[22] "A Quote by Virginia Satir." Goodreads.com, 2024, www.goodreads.com/quotes/447403-life-is-not-the-way-it-s-supposed-to-be-it-s. Accessed 8 Jan. 2026.

[23] "Og Mandino Quote." Lib Quotes, 2017, libquotes.com/og-mandino/quote/lby1j4e. Accessed 8 Jan. 2026.

[24] "A Quote by Mother Teresa." Goodreads.com, 2024, www.goodreads.com/quotes/820934-some-people-come-in-our-life-as-blessings-some-come.

[25] Global Desk. "Quote of the Day by Helen Keller: "the Best and Most Beautiful Things in the World Cannot Be Seen..." - In." The Economic Times, Economic Times, 27 Dec. 2025, economictimes.indiatimes.com/news/international/us/quote-of-the-day-december-27-quote-of-the-day-by-helen-keller-the-best-and-most-beautiful-things-in-the-world-cannot-be-seen-inspirational-words-by-the-first-deaf-blind-college-graduate/articleshow/126204709.cms. Accessed 8 Jan. 2026.

[26] "Quotes about Grief - 49 Quotes to Ease Loss- Craven Funerals." Cravens-Funerals.com, 2025, www.cravens-funerals.com/blog/quotes-about-grief-49-quotes-to-ease-loss/.

[27] Magazine, Education. "15 Grief Quotes That Speak to the Heart in Tough Times." The Education Magazine, 23 Apr. 2025, www.theeducationmagazine.com/word-art/grief-quotes/. Accessed 8 Jan. 2026.

[28] "Little by Little, We Let Go of the Loss...but Never of Love | VeeroesQuotes." VeeroesQuotes, 16 Mar. 2023, veeroesquotes.com/little-by-little-we-let/#google_vignette. Accessed 8 Jan. 2026.

[29] linepoetry. "Healing Grief Quotes: Comfort and Strength for Overcoming Loss." Linepoetry.com, 25 July 2024, linepoetry.com/healing-grief-quotes#google_vignette. Accessed 8 Jan. 2026.

[30-35] Chace, Keely. "75+ Grief Quotes to Give You Comfort and Help You Heal." Hallmark Ideas & Inspiration, May 2024, ideas.hallmark.com/articles/sympathy-ideas/comforting-grief-quotes/.